P9-EGL-644

Composer's World

Joseph Haydn

by Wendy Thompson

VIKING

*In memory of
Joy Campbell (1919–1991)*

Introduction

Of the three great Classical composers of the eighteenth century, who all lived and worked in and around Vienna, Joseph Haydn was the eldest and longest lived. He was born in 1732, when both Bach and Handel, the greatest composers of the Baroque era, were at the height of their fame; and he died in 1809, outliving his friend Mozart by eighteen years and having seen his greatest pupil, Beethoven, well established in his own career. But neither Mozart nor Beethoven could have created their masterpieces – symphonies, string quartets, sonatas – without the example of Haydn, who practically invented the Classical style in music as we know it.

Haydn's long life spanned a period not only of musical, but also of enormous social and political change. He was born at a time when Europe was ruled by great dynasties – the Hapsburgs in Austria, the Romanovs in Russia, the Hanovers in England, the Bourbons in France – together with a motley assortment of lesser princes in their own little kingdoms. Germany and Italy as we know them today did not exist; instead, there were many smaller states, each with its own ruler. There was no democracy – ordinary people had no say in how the state was run – nor was there any provision for "social security," old age pensions, or unemployment benefit. Life was hard for the majority of people, and especially for musicians, who worked in a very precarious profession. Many found employment as singers, composers, or instrumentalists either at a court or for a church or cathedral. Bach worked for the church of St. Thomas at Leipzig, while Mozart's father, Leopold – and at first, Mozart himself – worked for the Archbishop of Salzburg. In those days, of course, there was no television or cinema, so many aristocrats kept their own private orchestras to provide music for their entertainment. The system worked quite well, so long as the employer was kept happy and could afford to keep up his musical establishment. But the musicians – including composers – were treated as servants; they had to live in the servants' quarters, wear uniforms, and be constantly at their employer's beck and call. And unless the employer agreed, they could only write or perform music as required: they were generally not allowed to do "free-lance" work outside to earn more money.

Mozart eventually rebelled against this restrictive and

Wolfgang Amadeus Mozart (1756–1791)

Joseph Haydn

humiliating system, and tried to work for himself as a "free-lance." Haydn, however, spent most of his life in the service of one great princely family, the Esterházys. He was lucky: his employers recognized his talent and his value to them, and treated him well. But all his life, Haydn yearned for freedom: the kind of freedom which was only possible after the cataclysmic events of the French Revolution changed the structure of European society forever.

The Revolution proved that monarchs were only human after all: it abolished the great Bourbon dynasty which had been the envy of all other European kings and princes, and on which they had tried to model their own lifestyles. And the new battle cry of the middle and lower classes – "Liberty, Equality, Fraternity" – sent shivers of fear through the throne rooms of Europe. After 1789, nothing would be the same again. The Old Regime – under which the aristocracy held all the power, all the money, and enjoyed an unimaginably luxurious standard of living – was effectively finished. Those rulers who survived the wars and revolutions that marked the end of the eighteenth century were forced to cut back on spending; and many – including the Esterházy family – found that they could no longer afford such luxuries as a private orchesta. But again, Haydn was fortunate: his long service to the family did not go unrewarded, and he was pensioned off. This allowed him far more personal freedom in the last twenty years of his life: he was at last able to travel, and to enjoy the fruits of his success as the most famous composer of his time. And unlike poor Mozart, whose career had ended in poverty and an early death, Haydn reached the end of his long life in relative comfort, prosperity, and recognition.

1 From Cottage to Castle

Haydn was born on March 31, 1732, in the village of Rohrau, about fifty kilometres, or thirty-one miles, south-east of Vienna. This little corner of the Hapsburg Empire was peopled by a mixture of nationalities – Austrian, Hungarian, Moravian, Slovak, and Croatian – but the Haydn family seems to have been of German origin. Haydn's father, Mathias, was a wheelwright and the "market magistrate" of Rohrau: he had to keep an eye on the market and the state of the roads in the village. But although Mathias Haydn was quite an important man in local society, he and his wife Anna lived in a very modest cottage. There, twelve children were born, of whom, as was often the case, half died in infancy. Three girls, Francesca, Anna Maria, and Anna Katharina, survived; as did three boys, Joseph, Johann Evangelist, and Johann Michael. All the boys took up musical careers: Johann Michael eventually found a job as composer to the Archbishop of Salzburg, and became a great friend of the Mozart family.

Mathias Haydn loved music and used to sing folksongs, accompanying himself on the harp. By the time

Haydn's birthplace in Rohrau

The entry of Haydn's birth in the Rohrau parish register

Ansicht des Hauses in Rohr....

in welchem **Joseph Haydn** *im Jahre 1732 den 1 April und* **Michael Haydn** *im Jahre 1737 den 14ten September geboren worden sind.*

Michael Haydn (1737–1806)

Joseph was five, he too could sing his father's songs. When he was six, his uncle Johann Mathias Franck paid the Haydn family a visit. Franck was the headmaster of the school at Hainburg, a town about fifteen kilometres, or nine miles, away in the Danube valley; and he was also the organist and director of music at the largest church there. As the Haydns sat down for their usual Sunday singsong, Franck noticed that little Joseph had a very attractive voice, and that he pretended to accompany himself on an imaginary violin, keeping perfect time. Franck offered to take Joseph as a pupil at his school. Mathias and Anna Haydn were in no position to educate their children themselves, and were sure that this would give Joseph the chance he needed to make a good living later on; so although they were naturally upset to part with their little boy (whom they would hardly ever see again), Joseph was sent shortly afterward to the pretty town of Hainburg, nestling beneath the ruins of its historic castle.

Joseph's uncle proved a harsh teacher: he often beat the boys, and his wife neglected their appearance. Joseph, used to his mother's high standards of cleanliness, was ashamed of the stains on his clothes, and his unwashed face and hands. The routine at Franck's school was severe for such a young child: the boys had school lessons from seven until ten in the morning, followed by Mass at church. After lunch there were another three hours of schoolwork, followed by violin and clavier (harpsichord) lessons. Nevertheless, during his two years in Hainburg, Joseph learned much about music. Despite sometimes receiving "more thrashings than food," he appreciated the trouble that Franck had taken over him. "I shall always be grateful to that man for making me work so hard," he said later in life.

In 1740, the choirmaster of St. Stephen's Cathedral in Vienna, Karl Georg Reutter, paid a visit to Hainburg, on the lookout for talented boys for his choir. He heard Haydn sing, and was so impressed that he agreed to accept him as a choirboy. So shortly after his eighth birthday, young Joseph arrived in Vienna, the capital of the mighty Austrian Empire. He was to stay there for more than twenty years.

A view of Vienna in the eighteenth century

An Accurate Prospect of VIENNA, the Capital of German

2 Vienna

Vienna in the eighteenth century was a mixture of splendor and squalor: a city of wide streets, including the Neumarkt and the Graben; leafy parks and gardens such as the Glacis, the Augarten, and the Prater, and of magnificent palaces and lavishly furnished apartments, where the aristocracy lived in great affluence; entertaining, listening to music supplied by their own private orchestras, throwing sumptuous balls and parties, or gambling the nights away. Behind these same elegant façades, however, poorer people lived crowded together, renting drafty attics or damp basements in which to bring up their large families.

All this must have seemed very strange and exciting to a child from the provinces, but Haydn's everyday life was no easier than at his uncle's school. Reutter was an ambitious man, more interested in furthering his own career than in the education and welfare of his choirboys. The children were neglected and half-starved: all of them looked forward eagerly to the occasions when they were asked to sing at private concerts for wealthy people, for only then were they given enough food. "I loved these concerts so much that I tried to sing as beautifully as I could, to get myself invited," said Haydn later. And although Reutter promised to teach Haydn composition, "he gave me nothing except a lot of harsh treatment."

The choirboys had to work hard. They were required to sing High Mass every morning and Vespers every afternoon in the cathedral, and to sing at weddings, funerals, civic ceremonies, and special occasions at court. Their general education consisted only of religious instruction, Latin, mathematics, and writing, and they were taught singing, violin, and clavier. As for composition, Haydn later said that he had never had a proper teacher. "I started with the

Karl Georg Reutter (1708–1772)

St Stephen's Cathedral, Vienna

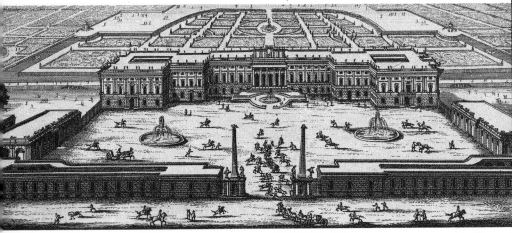

The Empress Maria Theresia (1717–1780)

practical side. . . I listened more than I studied, and tried to turn to good account the things which impressed me. I heard all the greatest music of my time, of which there was much in Vienna."

On several occasions, the choir was taken to perform at the palace of Schönbrunn, the magnificent, newly built home of the Empress Maria Theresia and her large family. On one such visit the boys began to play around on some scaffolding which was still erected round the walls. Distracted by the noise, the Empress herself came to a window and shouted that she would have them all whipped. But Haydn couldn't resist the temptation, and the next day he once again climbed the scaffolding. The Empress ordered that he should be given a sound thrashing – which Reutter promptly carried out.

By the time Joseph was in his early teens, his voice was beginning to break, and it became clear that he was no longer much use to the choir. "He sings like a crow," complained the Empress to Reutter. Things were made worse by the fact that Joseph's eight-year-old brother Michael had joined the choir, and sang like an angel, taking over all the solo parts that Joseph had once sung. Maria Theresia was

so delighted that she gave the younger boy a present of 24 golden ducats. It was not surprising that Joseph felt the need to draw attention to himself by playing silly pranks. In November 1749, he finally gave Reutter the chance to expel him by cutting off the pigtail of one of his fellow choristers with a pair of scissors. "I'd rather leave the choir than be beaten," he told Reutter. But the sadistic choirmaster promptly caned him soundly, and then threw him out into the street with no money and only the ragged clothes he stood up in.

By a stroke of luck, he met up with a young music teacher whom he knew. Johann Michael Spangler lived in a small garret with his wife and child, and generously offered to take the penniless young musician in. Haydn gratefully accepted the offer, and lived with the Spanglers for a few months. But then he had an unexpected windfall – a friend of his father's heard of his plight and lent him 150 florins (about $576 now), which must have seemed a small fortune. Haydn found himself a "miserable little attic room without a stove" in St. Michael's House, next to St. Michael's Church. The roof leaked, and he was cold, but he managed to buy himself an old harpsichord, and started to earn a meager living by singing as a tenor in the cathedral choir, doing a little teaching, and playing the violin for services at a nearby monastery, and for parties or private concerts in the evenings. When he was not working, he was studying music theory and writing his own music, especially piano sonatas for his pupils to play, trios, and dance music. And just as the young Mozart had learned a great deal about the art of composition from one of Bach's sons (Johann Christian), so Haydn learned a great deal from studying the keyboard sonatas of another Bach – Carl Philipp Emanuel. "I did not leave my keyboard until I had played through them, and those who know me well must realize how much I owe to Emanuel Bach," he said in later years.

Haydn also began to make some important contacts in society. One advantage of the Viennese lifestyle was that even a destitute young composer could easily meet his richer neighbors on the stairs. Haydn discovered that one of the tenants on the third floor of his lodging house was the great Italian writer Pietro Metastasio, who was at that time the Imperial Court Poet. Metastasio was the guardian of a young girl, and he engaged Haydn as her music teacher. She also took singing lessons from Nicola Porpora, another famous Italian musician working for the Viennese court. So Haydn met Porpora, and soon became his assistant and valet. "I learnt a great deal from Porpora in singing, in composition, and in speaking Italian," he recalled.

Nicola Porpora (1686–1768)

St. Michael's House in the Kohlmarkt

One of Haydn's earliest keyboard sonatas, in G major

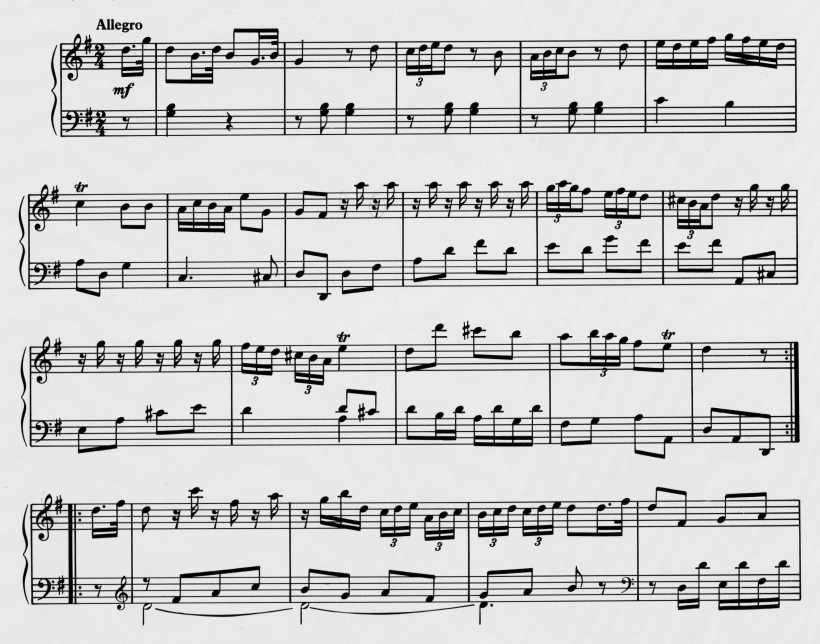

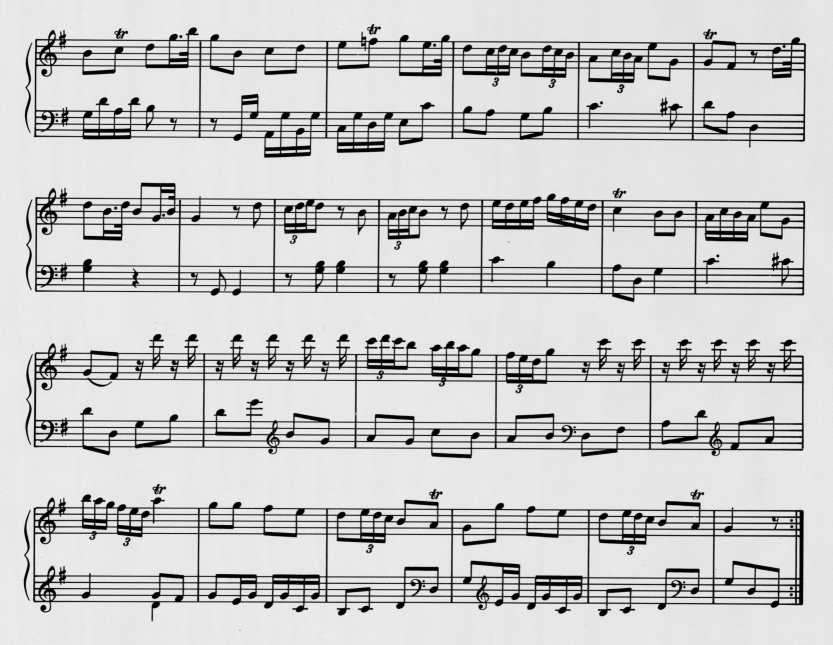

11

Haydn and his friends playing quartets

Through Porpora Haydn met several noblemen, including the music lover Karl Joseph von Fürnberg, who invited Haydn to his country house to play chamber music. There, Haydn wrote his first string quartets. Over the next fifty years, he was to develop the string quartet from a kind of music for light entertainment, in which the first violin had the most interesting and showy part, into a deeply serious form, in which all four instruments played an equal part. Mozart and Beethoven both modeled their own great quartets on those of Haydn.

In 1759, Haydn became music director to another nobleman, Count Karl Joseph Franz Morzin, who lived in Vienna during the winter and spent the summer at his country estate at Lukaveč in Bohemia. For the first time in his life, Haydn had a regular salary – 200 florins a year (about $810 now), plus his board and lodging. The Count kept his own orchestra at Lukaveč and Haydn had to supervise all the music. It was for this little orchestra of sixteen players that he wrote the first of his 106 symphonies. (Nowadays, it seems inconceivable that anyone could write so many symphonies, and Haydn was the last major composer to produce so many of these works – each one completely different in character.) This in turn led to another important contact: the symphony was heard by another, even more powerful nobleman, Prince Paul Anton Esterházy. The Prince was so charmed by the piece that he offered Haydn a post as his Kapellmeister (music director). Haydn accepted – but before taking up the post, he took a step which was to cause him much unhappiness for the rest of his life. He decided that he could afford to get married.

Like Mozart, Haydn fell in love with one girl, who turned him down, and then he married her sister. His first love was Josepha Keller, the daughter of a wigmaker. But Josepha was set on entering a convent; and perhaps out of a mistaken sense of duty, Haydn agreed to marry her elder sister, Maria Anna. The wedding took place on November 26, 1760, at St. Stephen's Cathedral (where Mozart and Constanze Weber were also to be married). But whereas Mozart's marriage was a very happy one, Haydn's was a disaster. His wife was bad-tempered, unattractive, and didn't care "whether her husband was a cobbler or an artist." Her only concern was for her duties to the church. Haydn was obliged to find happiness elsewhere: as he later explained, "My wife could not have children, and so I began to find other women attractive." And it seems that women found him attractive, too, although he was by no means handsome. He was small and sturdy, with a beaky nose, a complexion – like Mozart's – marred by smallpox, and bright, fiery eyes.

3 Eisenstadt

1761–1764

On May 1, 1761, Haydn signed a contract of employment with Prince Paul Anton Esterházy, one of Hungary's most wealthy and powerful noblemen. The family traced its origins back to the early seventeenth century, when Nikolaus Esterházy became leader of the Hapsburg party and Elector Palatine of Hungary. Through political intrigue and advantageous marriages, the Esterházys gained ever more land and money, until by the end of the century, they owned twenty-five castles and huge tracts of land. Prince Paul Anton had succeeded to the estate when he was twenty-four. He was a great music lover, and had established a permanent orchestra at the family seat, the castle of Eisenstadt (also known by its Hungarian name, Kismarton). The Prince treated his employees well, although he still addressed them in the humiliating "third person" – he would never say to them "You must do this," but "He must do this."

Haydn was to be second-in-command to the old Kapellmeister Gregor Joseph Werner, a composer mainly of church music. But Prince Esterházy wanted to expand his orchestra and the scope of musical activities at his court, especially in the field of opera and orchestral music, and he

A view of Eisenstadt

realized that Werner was not up to the task. However, out of consideration for the old Kapellmeister, Haydn was to defer to him in all matters relating to choral music, while having a free hand in instrumental and operatic projects.

Haydn's contract, which ran for three years, stipulated that he must behave and dress "as befits a house officer in a princely court"; avoid becoming too familiar with the musicians for whom he was responsible in order to keep their respect; train the singers; rehearse the orchestra; keep all the instruments and music in good condition; and settle any disputes among the musical staff. For this, his kind, easygoing nature was ideally suited, and several times he managed to intervene to prevent the Prince dismissing a musician. ("Anyone can see by the look of me that I am a good-natured sort of fellow," he said of himself.) He also agreed to compose music when required by the Prince, who would own everything he had written; he would not compose for anyone else without special permission, nor give away copies of his music. Every day at noon Haydn had to

The Esterházy castle at Eisenstadt

appear in livery (court uniform) before the Prince, who would tell him what music was necessary for the day's entertainment. The Prince could dismiss Haydn immediately if he failed to please; but if Haydn wished to leave, he had to give six months' notice. In return, he was paid an annual salary of 400 florins (about $1530 now), and he would be housed and fed.

The orchestra which Haydn inherited was small by today's standards: five violins or violas, one cello, one double bass, one flute, two oboes, two bassoons, two horns, and one timpani player. The Prince was very keen on string music, being himself a violinist and cellist: and the first works which Haydn wrote for him were three symphonies, called "Le Matin," "Le Midi," and "Le Soir" ("Morning," "Noon," and "Evening"). In order to please his new employer, Haydn included elaborate parts for solo violin and cello.

Unhappily, Prince Anton Esterházy did not live long enough to enjoy the work of his talented new composer. He died within a year, on March 18, 1762; and his middle-aged brother, Prince Nikolaus, succeeded to the title. The new Prince had even more grandiose plans than his brother for the social life of his court, and he soon acquired the title "the Magnificent." For his son's wedding celebrations in January 1763, he ordered a new, full-length opera from Haydn, based on the ancient legend of the tragic love story of Acis and Galatea. And over the next three years, he made constant demands on the skill of his court composer. Haydn produced a steady flow of new works: symphonies, string quartets, trios, and many other "occasional pieces" for the diversion of the Esterházy household. He also composed a number of concertos, including several for violin (written for the brilliant Italian leader of the orchestra, Luigi Tomasini), one for cello, and two for horn.

The opening of the C major Cello Concerto

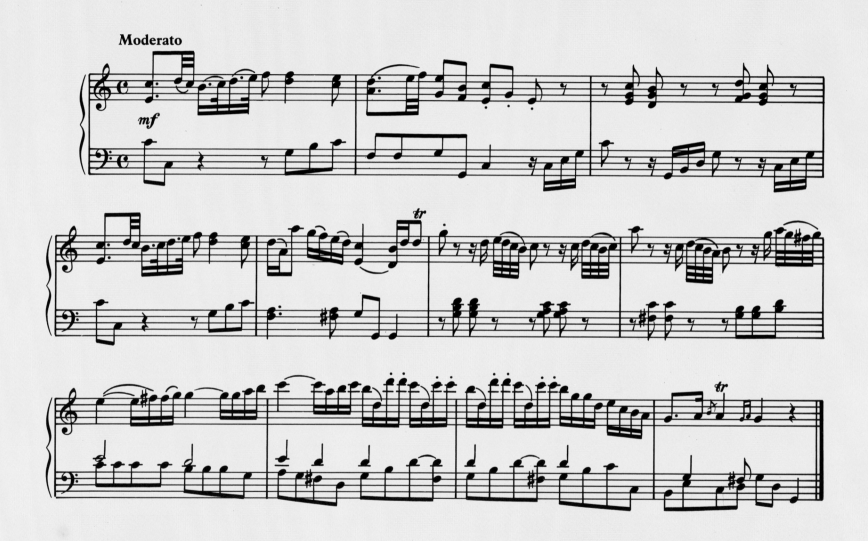

The Prince himself played an old-fashioned instrument called a baryton, which was related to the viol family. It had six strings played with a bow, together with others that vibrated freely in "sympathy" with the bowed notes, and was extremely difficult to master. But the Prince loved it, and over the next twelve years or so, Haydn turned out a huge amount of baryton music – about 160 pieces, including sonatas, duets, and trios with violin and cello. Haydn had to teach himself this strange and cumbersome instrument in order to compose for it; and then he found that the Prince was annoyed because Haydn could play it better than he could himself. Haydn quickly learned that diplomacy was the best policy, and decided to stick to composition.

Prince Esterházy's baryton

Prince Nikolaus Esterházy "the Magnificent"

16

Prince Nikolaus "the Magnificent" was determined to live up to his nickname. In 1764, he visited the French palace of Versailles, on which many other European monarchs, including the Hapsburgs, had modeled their own estates, and came home thoroughly dissatisfied with his splendid castle at Eisenstadt. For the "top league" of European royal families, one palace was simply not enough. In the days of Louis XIV, the French court moved around its many residences according to the seasons, spending the summers at Versailles, the winter at Saint Germain, and the hunting season down on the Loire. And many other monarchs had at least two palaces. (The Austrian Imperial family occupied the Hofburg Castle in Vienna during the winter, and built Schönbrunn as a summer residence; while the Romanovs in Russia had a Winter Palace in St. Petersburg and a summer palace in the country nearby.) The Esterházy family used to spend the winters in Vienna itself, and the summers at Eisenstadt; but Prince Nikolaus disliked Vienna. Inspired by the splendors of Versailles, he decided to build a sumptuous new summer palace. Just as Versailles itself had once been a hunting lodge on a marsh, the Prince's choice of site fell on a small hunting lodge situated on a boggy area of ground beside Lake Neusiedler. "He must be mad," thought the locals. But such was the wealth and resource of the Esterházy family that within just two years, the land had been drained and a magnificent palace was ready for occupation. It was called Eszterháza, and it cost 11 million florins (about $414 million now).

PROSPECT NACH DEM GARTEN UND WALD GEGEN SÜDEN.

The façade of Eszterháza in the eighteenth century

4 Eszterháza

Eszterháza was truly a fairytale palace. It had 126 guest rooms, a library containing 75,000 books, an art gallery filled with Old Masters, and two massive halls, both painted white with rich gilt decorations: one a concert hall and the other a ballroom. The Sala Terrena (a summer dining hall) had a white marble floor, while the Prince's suite was decorated with costly black-and-gold lacquered Japanese wallboards and contained an armchair which played music when anyone sat in it. There were many other rooms for displaying the Esterházy treasures: porcelain, magnificent furniture, and a collection of clocks, including one decorated with precious stones, its hands encrusted with diamonds.

The formal gardens were modeled on those at Versailles, with artificial waterfalls and fountains, terraces with orange trees in tubs (which in winter were kept in a specially heated winter garden), and alleys of linden and chestnut trees decorated with antique statues. There was an "amusement park" with charming little temples and a hermit's house, complete with model hermit. A Chinese House, built and decorated entirely in Chinese style, was known as "The Bagatelle." When the Empress Maria Theresia visited Eszterháza in 1773, she asked the Prince how much the Chinese House had cost to build, and he answered, with a dismissive wave of his hand, "Oh, a mere bagatelle"

A view of Eszterháza today

One of the reception rooms at Eszterháza

(a trifle). The separate stable block, the "Riding School," accommodated over 100 horses and a large number of splendid coaches.

In 1768, Prince Esterházy had a theater built in the grounds, to the west of the castle itself. It was some sixty feet wide and 180 feet long, two stories high, with a steeply sloping roof in the French style, and a façade decorated with classical columns. From the entrance hall a double staircase decorated with wrought-iron banisters led to the boxes and the gallery, from where the Prince and his personal guests watched the performances of plays and operas. The auditorium, which seated 400, was kept warm in winter by four huge stoves, with four more radiating heat from the basement through hot-air ducts. The stage itself incorporated all the most up-to-date machinery for scene changes.

The Prince demanded a theatrical performance every day. "The pleasures for the eyes and ears are indescribable," wrote a German visitor in 1783. "Herr Haydn, the Prince's court conductor, the world-famous composer, directs the orchestra, which plays perfectly. The excellent lighting effects and the superb decors are able to create the illusion of gods descending from heaven and afterwards ascending from the ground, then disappearing entirely, only to reappear again the next second; while a little later, you see a lovely garden or an enchanted forest changing into a magnificent hall."

For the opening of the theater in 1768, Haydn wrote a comic opera called *Lo speziale* ("The Apothecary"); and over the next fifteen years or so, he wrote about twelve operas for performance there. Many were written for special

An opera production at the Eszterháza theater in 1775: Haydn is at the keyboard

occasions, such as the marriages of members of the Prince's family, or the visit of the Archduke Ferdinand in 1775. "If I want to hear a good opera, I go to Eszterháza," said the Empress Maria Theresia, after attending a performance of one of Haydn's operas at the palace theater in 1773. But unlike Mozart's famous operas such as *The Marriage of Figaro*, *Don Giovanni*, and *The Magic Flute*, which are performed by opera companies all over the world, Haydn's operas are not so well known by modern audiences – and indeed Haydn himself admitted that his own operas could not stand comparison with Mozart's. Several years later, when he was invited to write an opera for Prague, he modestly turned the offer down, saying, "Why don't you ask Mozart?"

By 1773, Prince Esterházy was no longer satisfied with just one theater, and that year he added a marionette thea-

Costume designs for Haydn's opera "Armida"

20

The Music House at Eszterháza, where Haydn lived

ter, built to look like a magic grotto. "Opposite the opera you come across the spacious Puppet Theater. It has no boxes, or gallery, and its ground-floor auditorium seems to resemble a cave: the walls, the alcoves and openings are ornamented with different-colored stones, shells and snails. The puppets are finely made and dressed in fashionable costumes. Not only farces and fairytales, but also classical operas are performed here. It is quite unique, and the performances are open to all, free of charge," stated the official guidebook (written largely by Prince Esterházy himself!). For this little theater Haydn wrote another five or so puppet operas; and when the Opera House itself caught fire and burned down in November 1779 (a stove in the next-door Chinese Pavilion exploded), Haydn simply transferred all performances to the Puppet Theater, and carried on as if nothing had happened. (The Opera House itself was promptly rebuilt – even more lavishly – in exactly ten months.)

It was not surprising that the Prince found it difficult to tear himself away from all this splendor, and he began to spend most of his time at Eszterháza. Haydn was to spend well over twenty years there, working in relative isolation. He and his singers, musicians, actors, and actresses were housed in a separate building, the "Music House." Haydn was allowed married quarters (a three-room suite); but most of the other musicians were not allowed to bring their families to Eszterháza, and the long separation, often for up to ten months a year, together with the damp and unhealthy atmosphere of the surrounding swamplands, made them miserable.

But Haydn recognized that for him, the system had its advantages. "My Prince was always satisfied with my works," he wrote later. "I not only had the encouragement of his constant approval, but as conductor of the orchestra,

I could experiment, see what produced a good effect, and what spoilt it, and I was thus able to improve, alter, add or cut as boldly as I pleased. I was completely isolated from the world, there was no one to bother me, and I was forced to become original." The old Kapellmeister, Gregor Werner, had finally died in 1766, and from then on Haydn found himself in sole charge. He enlarged the orchestra to 22 players, and sent to Italy to recruit some of the finest singers of the time. Soon, the fame of the music at Eszterháza was spreading throughout Europe.

As well as operas, Haydn continued to write symphonies, chamber music, especially string quartets, and some church music. In the late 1760s, he produced a string of symphonies that were quite different from the lively, tuneful works of his youth. These pieces were written in unconventional keys, especially in the minor, which gave them a tragic, intense color; and were full of passionate, chromatic harmonies. Some of them have strange titles. For instance, No. 26, in D minor, is called "Lamentatione" ("Lamentations"); No. 49, in F minor, "La Passione" ("The Passion"); and No. 44, in E minor, the "Trauersinfonie" ("Mourning Symphony"). Haydn apparently asked that it should be played at his own funeral.

21

The opening of the "Trauersinfonie," No. 44

23

One explanation for this series of deeply emotional works – hardly suitable for light entertainment – was that Haydn had been influenced by a new cult in literature, called the "Sturm und Drang" ("storm and stress") style. This type of writing, dealing in gloomy subjects such as suicide, madness, and despair, was very popular among German writers of the time. The most famous of these was Johann Wolfgang von Goethe (1749–1832), whose writings influenced many important musicians, including Beethoven and Schubert, and it seems that Haydn, too, was affected by this fashionable gloom and doom.

The last piece he wrote in this style is perhaps the most famous. By November 1772, Prince Esterházy was showing no signs of wanting to leave Eszterháza, and the musicians of Haydn's orchestra, longing for their families and tired of hearing the wind howling across the desolate marshes, asked their popular Kapellmeister, whom they knew as "Papa Haydn," to help them. Instead of speaking directly to the

Johann Wolfgang von Goethe (1749–1832)

Haydn by C. L. Seehas

prince, Haydn decided to adopt a more subtle approach. His next piece was a symphony written in the extremely unusual key of F sharp minor, and at the end, Haydn added an extra, very slow movement. During this movement, each group of instruments – first the oboes, then the horns, then the bassoons and the double basses, and then each pair of string players – blew out their candles, took their instruments, and crept out. Finally only two violins were left playing – Haydn and Tomasini, the leader of the orchestra. When they had finished, they too blew out their candles and departed, leaving the Prince and his bewildered guests sitting alone in darkness. Fortunately the Prince took the hint. After the performance he told the orchestra, "Well, if you are going, we might as well all go," and the next day the Court packed up for Vienna. The symphony has ever after been known as the "Farewell." During these years Haydn also exploited the "Sturm und Drang" style in his other works, such as three sets of six string quartets, and in some of his piano sonatas, such as the great C minor Sonata of 1771. He also began to write church music, including a setting of the Latin hymn *Stabat mater* (relating the sorrow of the Virgin Mary as she stands beside the Cross), another hymn, *Salve regina* ("Hail, queen of heaven"), and four masses for the Catholic church service. These include the St. Cecilia Mass, written in honor of music's patron saint, the St. Nicholas Mass, written in 1772 for the name-day of his patron (all Catholics have a birthday, and a name-day, on which they celebrate the saint after whom they are named), and the Mass of St. John of God, known as the "Little Organ Solo Mass" because it includes a very complicated organ solo during the section called the Benedictus. And his patron began to allow him to write a few works for other people or organizations, such as the oratorio *The Return of Tobias*, written for the famous Society of Music in Vienna.

5 Later Years at Eszterháza

The demands made on Haydn's time and skills remained heavy at Eszterháza. Haydn had to rehearse the orchestra for two concerts a week, and prepare opera performances (in one year alone there were 125 performances of seventeen operas, eight of which were new works, though not all of these were by Haydn). Meanwhile, he continued to write new symphonies, and another set of six string quartets, which were later published as his Op. 33.

1779 was an important year for Haydn. He signed a new contract with his employer, which for the first time did not give the Prince exclusive rights over his works – so that he was now officially free to write for other people. He also bought a house in Eisenstadt, to live in during the winter months. And he fell in love – with a young Italian singer called Luigia Polzelli. Luigia and her husband Antonio, a violinist, were taken on at Eszterháza that year. Neither proved a very good artist, and within a year the Prince wanted to dismiss them; but Haydn intervened, because of his attachment to the nineteen-year-old singer, who seemed to be as unhappily married as he. So the Polzellis stayed, and Haydn seems to have caused quite a scandal by carrying on an affair with Luigia, under the noses of his wife and Luigia's husband. This continued until she went back to Italy after her husband's death in 1791; and even nine years later, when Haydn's own wife finally died (much to his relief), Luigia persuaded Haydn, who was nearly thirty years older than she, to sign a declaration that he would marry no one else but her. But in fact she married someone shortly afterward, whereas Haydn never remarried.

Around the same time, Haydn made an important business contact, with the Viennese publishing firm of Artaria. Up to then, only one work of Haydn's had been published

The Kohlmarkt in Vienna, showing Artaria's publishing house

with his permission, a set of six piano sonatas dedicated to Prince Esterházy. Since there was no copyright law in those days to protect composers' works, it is likely that some of Haydn's pieces had already been circulating in "pirated" editions abroad. But now, since the restrictions on his terms of employment had been relaxed, Haydn felt able to authorize Artaria to publish some of his works: string quartets, piano trios, and several symphonies. Artaria also issued two popular collections of Haydn's songs.

In 1784, Haydn wrote his last opera for the Eszterháza theater, the "heroic drama" *Armida*, a much more serious work than his earlier frothy comedies. Having neglected the concerto for many years, Haydn now produced two more a cello concerto for the orchestra's principal cellist, Anton Kraft, and a piano concerto in D. This is a delightful work, probably inspired by the brilliant piano concertos of Mozart, with a rondo finale in the "Hungarian" or "gypsy" style, which was very popular at the time. Many of Haydn's works have this special hint of "local color": he never forgot his peasant origins, and many of his themes draw on Austrian or Hungarian folksongs – the rough, gutsy "music of the people" that he heard as a child. It is this rustic flavor, pulsating with rhythmic energy and enlivened by many deft touches of wit and humor, that distinguishes much of his music from the suave, elegant, polished style of Mozart, although both composers fashioned their works from the kind of musical material that we recognize as belonging to the Classical style.

"Hungarian Rondo" from the Piano Concerto in D major

An engraving of Haydn in middle age

A Masonic meeting in Vienna

In early 1785, Haydn, like Mozart, became a Freemason at a Viennese Lodge. Although he didn't stay in the Order for very long, this was an important social step to take: many of the most influential people in Vienna, including Prince Esterházy himself, were Freemasons. Some time before then, Haydn must have met and become friends with the young genius from Salzburg, who was currently enjoying a great deal of success in Vienna as a performer and composer. Haydn and Mozart sometimes played chamber music together – Haydn on the violin and Mozart on the viola – and Mozart was so impressed by Haydn's string quartets that in 1785 he dedicated a set of six quartets of his own to Haydn, saying, "I send my six sons to you, most celebrated and very dear friend. . . Your good opinion encourages me to offer them to you in the hope that you will not consider them unworthy of your favor." Haydn, in return, told Leopold Mozart that his son was "the greatest composer known to me either personally or by reputation. He has taste, and, what is more, the most profound knowledge of composition." Later, he wrote, "If I could tell every music lover and especially the chief musicians of today what I feel

An unfinished portrait of Mozart by Joseph Lange

about Mozart's inimitable works, their depth of emotion and their unique musical quality, every nation would be fighting to own such a great talent."

As a result of the many publications of Haydn's music, his reputation had by now spread all over Europe. In late 1784 or early 1785, he received an important request from a Parisian Masonic Lodge, the "Olympique," for six symphonies. These pieces, known now as the "Paris" Symphonies, form Nos.82 to 87 in Haydn's catalogue, and they have nicknames such as "L'Ours" ("The Bear"), "La Poule" ("The Hen"), and "La Reine" ("The Queen") – so called because it was apparently one of Queen Marie Antoinette's favorite works. Haydn couldn't go to Paris for the performance, but the new symphonies were a great success with the French public, and Haydn was soon asked to write another set of three (Nos.90–92).

Symphony No. 85 ("La Reine")

Also in 1785, Haydn received another, rather unusual commission from Cádiz Cathedral in Spain. He was asked to compose some instrumental music to accompany the "Seven Last Words of Our Savior From the Cross," to be performed at a special service on Good Friday. Haydn's seven slow movements, scored for a larger than usual orchestra, were later adapted for string quartet, the version in which they are normally played today. Haydn was paid for the work with a large chocolate cake filled with gold coins.

By 1789, the year of the French Revolution, Haydn was fed up with the restrictions of his life at Eszterháza, where he was still treated as a servant – a valued one, but with no personal freedom. "Art is free," he wrote. "It is a

sad thing always to be a slave." And to his great friend Marianne von Genzinger, the wife of one of Prince Esterházy's personal doctors, he wrote complaining about his enforced return to his "wilderness" after a jolly New Year spent among friends in Vienna. "Here I sit, forsaken, like a poor orphan, with no one to talk to, melancholy, full of memories of past glorious days. . . I couldn't sleep, and just when I was dreaming that I was hearing *The Marriage of Figaro*, I was awakened by that dreadful North wind nearly blowing my nightcap off my head." At Eszterháza, grumbled Haydn, he was obliged to eat "fifty-year-old chunks of cow," an "old sheep with carrots," nuts, and dry apple fritters. "Here no one asks me 'Would you like some chocolate, with or without milk? How do you like your coffee, black or with cream? What would you like, my dear Haydn? Would you care for a vanilla or a pineapple ice?' If only I had a nice piece of Parmesan cheese, so that I could swallow those black dumplings and noodles more easily. . ."

During his last years at Eszterháza, Haydn turned once more to string quartets. In 1787, Artaria published another set of six, known as the "Prussian" Quartets, Op.50, since they were dedicated to the King of Prussia. And toward the end of the 1780s, Haydn wrote two more sets of six quartets for Johann Tost, a violinist in the Esterházy orchestra, who later married a rich wife and set up in business in Vienna. These works, Opp.54–5 and Op.64, are known as the "Tost" Quartets. The second of the Op.55 set, in F minor, is known as the "Razor" Quartet. The story goes that a London publisher, John Bland, visited Haydn in 1789, looking for new pieces. When he arrived, Haydn was having trouble shaving. "I'll give my best quartet for a new razor," he exclaimed; whereupon Bland gave him his own set of steel razors. And in return, Haydn gave Bland the manuscript of the F minor Quartet.

Haydn by John Hoppner (1792)

6 Freedom

In September 1790, as the Old Regime began to crumble, Haydn's employer Prince Nikolaus Esterházy (who had certainly enjoyed all of its benefits), died at the age of seventy-seven. His son and successor, Anton, had inherited none of his father's love for the arts. He immediately dismissed the orchestra and the choir at Eszterháza, and shortly afterward abandoned the palace as well. The Austro-Hungarian Empire was currently involved in a long and costly war against the Turkish Empire; and many aristocrats found that the war effort drained their purses. Within a few decades, the beautiful theaters at Eszterháza had become storerooms, and by 1900 the once-lovely palace was a ruin. (It has recently been restored to most of its former glory.)

While the orchestra and singers lost their jobs, Haydn was allocated a generous annual pension of 1400 florins (about $5580 now) in recognition of many years of faithful service to the family. But although his official duties were now over, he was still technically a servant of the Prince and had to ask permission before he could work for anyone else.

Shortly after arriving back in Vienna, Haydn was offered another job – as court composer to the King of Naples, for whom he had written some pieces several years before for the King's favorite instrument, a kind of hurdy-gurdy called the "lyra organizzata." But after his years of being "buried alive" at Eszterháza, Haydn was in no hurry to take up another similar position, and he declined the offer. Soon afterward, he was visited by a well-known violinist, Johann Peter Salomon, who had worked all over Europe, leading orchestras and promoting concerts in Paris and London. Salomon proposed to take Haydn back with him to London, and made him a tempting offer: $2160 for a

Johann Peter Salomon (1745–1815) by Thomas Hardy

new opera, six symphonies, and several other works. Haydn signed the contract the next day. Salomon also wanted to entice Mozart to London, and the younger composer – for whom things were not going at all well – agreed to come the following season (by which time he was too ill to go). The parting between the two friends was a very emotional one. Mozart, probably afraid that the elderly Haydn might not survive the arduous journey by land and sea, embraced him tearfully, saying, "I fear that we shall never see each other again." But in fact, it was Mozart – aged only thirty-five – who was to die the following year. Haydn, who heard the sad news in London, was deeply upset. "I was beside

myself," he wrote to a friend in Vienna. "I could not believe that Fate would cut short the life of such an indispensable man so soon."

Meanwhile Haydn – who had never before ventured outside Austria, except to Eszterháza, and who couldn't speak a word of English – traveled to London. The perilous journey, which took him through revolutionary France, lasted just over two weeks. Haydn, who had never seen the sea, found the ten-hour crossing of the English Channel rather terrifying. "I stayed on deck the whole time, so as to gaze my fill at that mighty monster, the ocean," he wrote to his friend Marianne von Genzinger. "I wasn't afraid so long as it was calm, but towards the end, when the wind grew much stronger and I saw the huge waves rushing at us, I became a little frightened, and a bit indisposed too. But I got over it, and arrived safely on shore. . ."

Mozart by Doris Stock

33

VIEW of LONDON from Greenwich Park.

noisy and expensive. He was asked to write an opera, though for some reason it was never performed in London. But he did write two new symphonies for Salomon's next series of concerts at the famous Hanover Square Concert Rooms, at that time London's major concert hall, seating 800. Salomon led the orchestra, and Haydn followed his customary practice by sitting at the keyboard and filling in some of the harmonies. Haydn's pieces received rave reviews in the press. "A new grand overture (the Symphony No.96) by Haydn was received with the highest applause, and universally deemed a composition as pleasing as scientific," reported one newspaper after the first concert on March 11, 1791. "The first movement in particular rises in grandeur of subject, and in the rich variety of *air* and passion, beyond any even of his own productions," stated the *Morning Chronicle*. "The Overture has four movements – an Allegro—Andante—Minuet and Rondo. They are all beautiful, but the first is pre-eminent in every charm and the Band performed it with admirable correctness. . ."

Haydn's arrival in Georgian London caused a sensation and he was the talk of the town. "I could dine out every day if I wanted to," he wrote, "but I have to consider my health and my work." Shortly after his arrival, he was visited by the ambassadors of both Austria and Naples, and on January 19, he was invited to the Royal Court Ball to celebrate Queen Charlotte's birthday. There he was introduced to the Prince of Wales, the future King George IV, at that time leader of the most fashionable social set in London. The Prince immediately invited Haydn to take part in a musical evening at his residence, Carlton House, in Pall Mall.

Haydn found London immensely stimulating, but very

Carlton House, the Prince of Wales' residence in Pall Mall

Left: *A view of eighteenth-century London from Greenwich Park*

Hanover Square in 1750

Hanover Square Concert Rooms

In July 1791, Haydn was invited to Oxford to receive the honorary degree of Doctor of Music. As part of his "doctoral exercise," he submitted the Symphony No.92 (originally written in 1789), and it has ever since been known as the "Oxford." At the degree ceremony he wore his academic gown of cream- and cherry-colored silk, and as the audience applauded, he turned and thanked them in English. He was, however, appalled by the cost of the ceremony: "1½ guineas for having the bells rung and ½ guinea for the robe," plus a further four guineas in travelling expenses.

For his two seasons of London concerts, 1791–2 and 1794–5, Haydn composed his last twelve symphonies, Nos. 93–104, a brilliant series known as the "London" symphonies. Some of them have nicknames: No.96, the "Miracle," has for some unknown reason been wrongly connected with an incident which took place in 1794, when another of Haydn's symphonies, No.102, was being played. A heavy cut-glass chandelier crashed down from the ceiling into the crowded hall: but because the audience had all pressed forward to the front to cheer Haydn, mercifully no one was injured! No.94 is known as the "Surprise": the story goes that Haydn was so annoyed by the fact that so many members of the audience appeared to fall asleep during the slow movements of his symphonies, that in this one, in the middle of a drowsily innocent little tune, he suddenly introduced a loud crash on all the instruments, in order to jolt his patrons awake! At the first performance of No.100, the "Military," "the middle movement was again received with absolute shouts of applause," reported the *Morning Chronicle*. "Encore! encore! encore! encore! resounded from every seat: the Ladies themselves could not forbear. It is the advancing to battle; and the march of men, the sounding of the charge, the thundering of the onset, the clash of arms, the groans of the wounded, and what may be called the hellish roar of war increase to a climax of horrid sublimity!" No.101 is known as the "Clock," owing to the "ticking" motif of its slow movement; while No.103 has been dubbed the "Drum-Roll" – for obvious reasons. Haydn's last symphony, No.104, is called the "London."

Slow movement of the "Surprise" Symphony, No. 94

During his stay in England, Haydn made notes on all the places he visited and the curious customs of the British. Facts and figures fascinated him. "During the last 31 years, 38,000 houses were built in London." – "On 5th Nov. the boys celebrate the day on which the Guys set the town on fire." – "In the year 1791, 22,000 people died in London." – "In the month of January 1792, a roasting chicken cost 7 shillings, a turkey 9 shillings, a dozen larks 1 crown. NB a duck, if it is plucked, costs 5 shillings."

In November 1791, Haydn was invited to stay with the Prince of Wales and his brother the Duke of York, at Oatlands in Surrey, the Duke's beautiful country estate. There he was treated not as a servant, but as an esteemed and honored guest. "Oh, my dear good lady, how sweet is some degree of freedom," he wrote to his friend Marianne von Genzinger. "I had a good employer, but I was sometimes forced to depend on base persons. I often sighed for release, and now I have it. . ." In June 1792, Haydn visited the famous astronomer William Herschel in his laboratory at Slough. "I saw the great telescope," he reported. "It is forty feet long and five feet in diameter." On June 14, he went to Ascot to see the races: he was intrigued by the weighing-in system, and the betting. "The riders are clad very lightly in silk, each one in a different color, no boots, little caps on their heads, they are all as thin as greyhounds, like their horses. . . . The horses are of the finest possible breed, delicate, with very slender legs, their manes plaited, their hooves very small. As soon as they hear the bell, they dash off at once at great speed. Every stride of the horses is twenty-two feet long. They are very expensive. The Prince of Wales paid £8000 for one some years ago, and sold it again for £6000; but he won £50,000 with it the first time."

At the end of June 1792, Haydn left London and returned to Vienna. He must have been sorry to leave:

Oatlands, the Duke of York's country seat

The Oatland Stakes at Ascot, June 1791

during his stay he had formed a deep attachment to a widow called Rebecca Schroeter, who took piano lessons from him, and who quickly fell in love with both the man and his music. Haydn dedicated to Rebecca three of his finest piano trios, including the famous "Gypsy Rondo," and his three last piano sonatas. Years later, Haydn confessed to a friend that Rebecca "was a very attractive woman, and still handsome though over sixty; and had I been free I should certainly have married her."

On his way back, Haydn stopped at Bonn, where he was introduced to a young would-be composer called Ludwig van Beethoven. Haydn was so impressed that he offered to accept the stubborn, unruly young man as his pupil in Vienna. The relationship, even for such a genial teacher as Haydn, was a difficult one; and Haydn found himself seriously embarrassed when, hoping to do his penniless young pupil a good turn, he wrote to Beethoven's employer, the Elector of Cologne, asking for an increase in Beethoven's allowance, and sending him some examples of his pupil's "recent" compositions. The Elector replied icily that Beethoven had been allocated far more than the 100 ducats he claimed, and that almost all the compositions, far from being new, had been played in Bonn before Beethoven left to continue his studies in Vienna.

Haydn had hoped to take Beethoven with him when he returned to London in January 1794, but he decided against it. During his second season there, which was even more successful than his first, his latest set of string quartets, Op.71, were played at Salomon's concerts, and they were evidently written with the brilliant violinist's talents in mind. His last three symphonies were played at a new concert series, the Opera Concerts, in the King's Theater in the Haymarket, to rapturous acclaim. "What shall we say of Haydn and the sublime, the magic Overture (symphony)

The young Beethoven

The King's Theater in the Haymarket

with which he began the second act?" enthused the *Morning Chronicle*. He was also presented at court, and the music-loving King, George III, tried very hard to persuade him to stay in England. Queen Charlotte even offered him a suite in Windsor Castle! But the sixty-three-year-old composer decided that he wanted to end his life in his native land. On his last benefit concert, he made 4000 florins on one evening alone. "Such a thing is only possible in England."

Soon Haydn learnt that Prince Anton Esterházy had died, and the new Prince, Nikolaus II, wanted to start up the music at his court again, with Haydn as Kapellmeister. So in August 1795, Haydn returned to Vienna, about $2700 the richer overall for his "English experience."

A view of Windsor Castle in the eighteenth century

Haydn by George Dance (1794)

7 Last Years

In May 1791, Haydn had attended a vast Handel Festival in Westminster Abbey, at which *Messiah* was performed. He was deeply moved by the experience, especially by the great "Hallelujah" Chorus. "Here is the master of us all!" he said of Handel.

Back at Eisenstadt, where Prince Nikolaus Esterházy had re-established his court, he found that his new patron disliked instrumental music. The only duty he required of his Kapellmeister was that he should compose a mass each year, for the name-day of Princess Maria Hermenegild, the Prince's wife. Haydn had not written any masses for over fourteen years; but between 1796 and 1802 he duly produced six – and these are among his greatest compositions: they use a large orchestra and are scored with brilliance and vigor. Although they are sacred music, Haydn drew on all the resources of his experience in the fields of opera and the symphony.

Two of these masses refer directly to the political situation. France, under the leadership of the ambitious young Corsican general Napoleon Bonaparte, had emerged from the horrors of the Revolution only to be plunged into war against virtually every other European state. The first of Haydn's masses, dating from 1796, is known as the "Missa in tempore belli" ("Mass in time of war"). At the end, during the Agnus Dei (the closing prayer for peace), Haydn introduces the sound of far-off trumpets and drums – the menacing noises of warfare – to remind his listeners of their peril. And the third mass, written in 1798, is subtitled "Missa in angustiis" ("Mass in time of need"), and it also refers to the growing international tension. In that year the British admiral Lord Nelson defeated the French fleet at the Battle of the Nile, and Haydn's Mass has ever afterward

Prince Nikolaus Esterházy II

been known as the "Nelson" Mass. In 1800, Haydn was visited by Nelson and his beautiful mistress Lady Emma Hamilton, who was herself a fine singer. Nelson gave Haydn a gold watch as a memento, and Haydn gave Nelson his pen.

Mass No.2, written in 1796, is known in Germany as the "Heiligmesse" ("Holy Mass"); and No.4, written in 1799, as the "Theresienmesse" ("Theresia Mass"). No.5, which dates from 1801, is known as the "Creation" Mass, since it uses a theme from Haydn's own oratorio *The Creation*; and the last is the "Harmoniemesse" ("Wind-band Mass"), so-called because of the prominence which Haydn

The Battle of the Nile, August 1, 1798

*Lord Nelson
(1758–1805)*

gives to the wind instruments. "I am rather proud of my masses," said Haydn.

Haydn was also inspired by Handel's example to turn to the oratorio. Before he left England, he had been given a text based on Milton's epic poem *Paradise Lost*, and in 1797 and 1798 he was totally absorbed in writing a massive choral work based on a German translation of the poem, describing the creation of the world. "I was never so devout as when I wrote *The Creation*," he said. "I knelt down every day to pray to God to give me strength for my work." Even so, Haydn never lost his earthy sense of humor, and he must have thoroughly enjoyed himself depicting in music the various forms of divine handiwork which preceded the serious business of Man's creation, from leaping tigers and prancing horses down to the wrigglings of the humble earthworm! *The Creation*, which contains some of Haydn's loveliest arias and his most stirring choruses, such as "The heavens are telling," was first performed at the end of April 1798, at Prince Schwarzenberg's palace in Vienna. A year later it received its first public performance. The huge audience listened throughout in respectful silence to this masterpiece from the sixty-six-year-old composer. In 1800, it was performed in London with great success at Covent Garden Theater, and also in Paris, where Napoleon (a great admirer of Haydn) would have attended it had someone not tried to assassinate him on his way to the theater.

42

"The Heavens are Telling" from "The Creation"

At much the same time, Haydn also wrote two more of his most famous pieces. One was the popular Trumpet Concerto, written in 1796 for a newly developed instrument, the keyed trumpet. The other was once more inspired by an English model – the National Anthem. Haydn's wonderfully simple setting of the hymn "God save the Emperor Franz" was immediately taken up as the Austrian National Anthem, which it remained until the fall of the Hapsburg dynasty during the First World War. The delighted Emperor presented Haydn with a gold snuffbox; and Haydn used the melody as the theme for a set of variations in one of his string quartets, Op.76, No.3 known as the "Emperor" Quartet.

The "Emperor's Hymn"

The house where Haydn died in Vienna

In 1800, Haydn was finally released from his long and unhappy marriage by his wife's death – but by then he was too old to think of remarrying. Some time earlier he had bought himself a house in a suburb of Vienna: the street is now called the Haydngasse. There he enjoyed a regular routine, rising early, teaching and composing in the mornings, taking lunch between 2 and 3 PM, working again in the afternoons, going out in the evenings, and dining on a light supper of bread and wine at 10 PM. By 11:30 he would be in bed. Encouraged by the success of *The Creation*, Haydn spent the summer of 1800 at Eisenstadt, working on a new oratorio, *The Seasons*, which portrays a year's cycle in the life of the countryside. It was first performed privately on April 24, 1801, at the Schwarzenberg Palace, and in public at the Redoutensaal later the same month. But although it made Haydn a great deal of money, it wore him out. "I shouldn't have written it," he said.

And he composed very little more during the last six years of his long life: some Scottish folksong arrangements for a publisher in Edinburgh (in fact, many of them were written by one of his pupils, but they still became very popular), and his last string quartet, Op.103, which remained unfinished. Although the Esterházy family looked after him well, sending their own doctors to care for him, his health slowly deteriorated: when he didn't want to see any visitors he sent them a "visiting card," on which was written a short fragment of music with the words "Gone is all my strength, Old and weak am I." But honors were showered on him from royalty; and in 1804, the year he finally resigned his official post to the Esterházy family, he was granted the freedom of the city of Vienna.

Haydn's visiting card

45

"The Creation" performed at Vienna University, 1808

Haydn last appeared in public on March 27, 1808, at a performance of *The Creation* in honor of his seventy-sixth birthday in the Great Hall of Vienna University. He was so overcome by the occasion, on which he was cheered loudly by the large and distinguished audience, that he had to be taken home in the interval.

In May 1809, Napoleon's troops had reached the gates of Vienna, and began a massive artillery bombardment. A shell fell near Haydn's house, terrifying the servants, but the composer himself was too ill and exhausted to care. When the French army occupied the city, Napoleon had a guard of honor placed outside Haydn's door. The old man finally died on May 31, and was buried very quietly the next day in his local cemetery. Unlike Mozart, however, he was not forgotten. Two weeks later, the "whole art-loving world of Vienna" turned out to a great memorial service at a church in the city center. "Everything was very solemn, and worthy of Haydn," observed a mourner. And in 1820, Haydn's remains were exhumed and taken to the Bergkirche in Eisenstadt, where he lies under the protection of the noble family for whom he wrote so much glorious music.

The bombardment of Vienna, 1809

46

Glossary of Musical Terms

Opera A play set to music, usually in several acts. Most eighteenth-century operas were sung in Italian.

Oratorio A large-scale work for voices and orchestra, dealing with a religious subject.

Cantata A small-scale work for voice(s) and orchestra.

Mass A musical setting of the Catholic service, in Latin, for church use.

Minuet A courtly, graceful dance, much used for short piano pieces, or as one section of a larger orchestral piece.

Sonata A piece for one or two instruments (such as piano alone, or violin and piano) in several sections (called "movements").

Symphony A large-scale orchestral piece, usually in four separate sections (movements). The first and last were usually quick; the second slow, and the third was often a minuet (see above).

Concerto A piece, often in three movements, for a solo instrument and orchestra, intended to show off the soloist's technique. The first and third movements were normally fast, and the middle one slow.

Sinfonia Concertante "Concerted symphony." A cross between concerto and symphony,

Chamber Music Pieces for a small, but varied group of instruments, each playing an individual part.

Duet A piece of chamber music for two instruments.

Trio A piece of chamber music for three instruments.

Quartet A piece of chamber music for four instruments (a string quartet consisted of two violins, viola, and cello).

List of Works

Haydn wrote a huge amount of music. Some pieces which are said to be by him may be by other composers. It is not possible to list his works exactly. The following are his most important surviving compositions:

Operas
25, including *Lo speziale* ("The Apothecary," 1766), *Le pescatrici* ("The Fisherwomen," 1769), *L'infedeltà delusa* ("Unfaithfulness Deluded," 1773), *L'incontro improvviso* ("The Unexpected Meeting," 1775), *Il mondo della luna* ("The World on the Moon," 1777), *La vera constanza* ("True Constancy," 1778), *L'isola disabitata* ("The Desert Island," 1779), *La fedeltà premiata* ("Faithfulness Rewarded," 1780), *Orlando Paladino* ("Orlando the Knight," 1782), *Armida* (1784), *L'anima del filosofo* ("The Philosopher's Soul," 1791).

Masses
15, including *Grosse Orgelmesse* ("Great Organ Mass," 1768), *St. Cecilia Mass* (1766), *St. Nicholas Mass* (1772), *Kleine Orgelmesse* ("Little Organ Mass," 1775), *Missa in tempore belli* ("Mass in Time of War," 1796), *Heiligmesse* ("Holy Mass," 1796), *Missa in angustiis* ("Nelson Mass," 1798), *Theresienmesse* ("Theresia Mass," 1799), *Schöpfungsmesse* ("Creation Mass," 1801), *Harmoniemesse* ("Windband Mass," 1802).

Cantatas and Oratorios
Applausus (1768), *The Return of Tobias* (1774–5), *The Seven Last Words of Our Savior on the Cross* (1785), *The Creation* (1797–8), *The Seasons* (1798–1801).

Vocal Music
Songs for various combinations of voices, including 12 canzonettas to English words; 400 arrangements of British folk-songs; 52 original songs to German words.

Orchestral
Around 106 symphonies, including Nos.6 in D, 7 in C and 8 in G ("Le Matin," "Le Midi," "Le Soir"), No.22 in E flat ("The Philosopher"), No.26 in D minor ("Lamentatione"), No.31 in D ("Horn Signal"), No.44 in E minor ("Trauer-

sinfonie"), No.45 in F sharp minor ("Farewell"), No.48 in C ("Maria Theresia"), No.49 in F minor ("La Passione"), No.53 in D ("The Imperial"), No.55 in E flat ("The Schoolmaster"), No.59 in A ("Fire"), No.60 in C ("Il Distratto"), No.63 in C ("La Roxolane"), No.73 in D ("La Chasse"), Nos. 82–87 ("Paris" Symphonies), including No.82 in C ("L'Ours" – "The Bear"), No.83 in G minor ("La Poule" – "The Hen"), No.85 in B flat ("La Reine" – "The Queen"), No.92 in G ("Oxford"), Nos. 93–104 ("London" Symphonies), including No.94 in G ("Surprise"), No.96 in D ("Miracle"), No.100 in G ("Military"), No.101 in D ("Clock"), No.104 in D ("London").

Many overtures, minuets, marches, German dances, etc. for orchestra.

Concertos, including 3 for violin, 2 for cello, 6 for keyboard, 1 for horn, 5 for lyra organizzata, 1 for trumpet, *Sinfonia concertante* for oboe, bassoon, violin, and cello.

Chamber Music

68 string quartets; 32 piano trios; 21 or more divertimentos for string trio; 126 baryton trios; 11 pieces for mechanical clocks; 53 piano sonatas.

The author wishes to acknowledge her debt to many sources, including *The Great Composers: Haydn* by H. C. Robbins Landon (Faber & Faber 1972), *The Collected Correspondence and London Notebooks of Joseph Haydn* ed. Robbins Landon (Barrie & Jenkins 1959), *Joseph Haydn* (Grove 6) and *Haydn* by Neil Butterworth (Omnibus Press, 1983).

Picture Credits

The author and publishers have made every effort to identify the owners of the pictures used in this publication; they apologize for any inaccuracies and would like to thank the following
(*a: left, b: right*):

Historisches Museen der Stadt Wien 4, 45b.
Bild-Archiv der Österreichischen Nationalbibliothek Wien 9b, 14, 26, 46a, 46b.
Sammlungen der Gesellschaft der Musikfreunde in Wien 16b.
Internationale Stiftung Mozarteum Salzburg 28c.
Mit genehmigung des Beethoven-Hauses Bonn 39a.
Reproduced by gracious permission of Her Majesty the Queen 31
The Royal College of Music, London frontispiece, 32, 33b, 36b, 40b.
Reproduced by kind permission of The Witch Ball 39b.
Reproduced by courtesy of the Trustees of the British Museum 42a.
ET Archive 5, 7a (Gesellschaft der Musikfreunde in Wien), 8b, 28b (Historisches Museen der Stadt Wien), 29 (Victoria & Albert Museum, London), 13 (The National Gallery of Budapest), 42b.
The Bridgeman Art Library 25 (Schwerin Museum, Germany).
Author's collection 2, 3, 6, 7b, 8a, 12, 24, 28a, 33a, 34, 35a, 35b, 36a, 38a, 38b, 40a, 45a.

The cover shows a portrait of Haydn by Güttenbrun (private collection of Mrs Eva Alberman, reproduced by permission of ET Archive) against the Eszterháza palace and an engraving of Fenchurch Street, London.

VIKING
Published by the Penguin Group
Viking Penguin, a division of Penguin Books USA Inc., 375 Hudson Street, New York, New York 10014, U.S.A.
Penguin Books Ltd, 27 Wrights Lane, London W8 5TZ, England
Penguin Books Australia Ltd, Ringwood, Victoria, Australia
Penguin Books Canada Ltd, 2801 John Street, Markham, Ontario, Canada L3R 1B4
Penguin Books (N.Z.) Ltd, 182—190 Wairau Road, Auckland 10, New Zealand

Penguin Books Ltd, Registered Offices: Harmondsworth, Middlesex, England

First published in Great Britain by Faber Music Ltd in association with Faber and Faber Ltd, 1991

First American edition published in 1991

10 9 8 7 6 5 4 3 2 1

Copyright © Wendy Thompson, 1991
All rights reserved

Library of Congress Catalog Card Number: 91—50212

ISBN 0-670-84171-4

Printed in Spain

Set in Sabon Roman

Without limiting the rights under copyright reserved above, no part of this publication may be reproduced, stored in or introduced into a retrieval system, or transmitted, in any form or by any means (electronic, mechanical, photocopying, recording or otherwise), without the prior written permission of both the copyright owner and the above publisher of this book.